JN088914

Ultra-basic Level

Read on, Think on
［入門］考える基礎英語読本

Jonathan Lynch / Atsuko Yamamoto / Kanako Watanabe

SANSHUSHA

音声ダウンロード＆ストリーミングサービス（無料）のご案内

https://www.sanshusha.co.jp/onsei/isbn/9784384335026/

本書の音声データは、上記アドレスよりダウンロードおよびストリーミング再生ができます。ぜひご利用ください。

Download

Streaming

Preface

　英語学習はたやすいものではなく、学習意欲を持続させることはむずかしいものです。学習者が自分のペースで学習したいと思っていても、ときとして学校での学習プランが自分のペースより速かったり、教材が難しすぎて、すぐに理解不能に陥り、やる気をなくしてしまうこともあります。そこで、以下の点に留意した比較的ゆっくりとしたペースで学びたい英語初級者のためのリーディング教材を作成しました。

1. 英文の長さを 250 words 前後にしぼりました。
2. 内容は学生に関係があり、面白く読めるものにしました。
3. 単語レベルを頻出単語にしぼり初心者でも読めるような英文にしました。
4. 学習者の学習意欲を高めるような読解問題、単語問題、文法問題などを用意しました。
5. 学習者の理解度を高めるために日本語を一部使用しました。

　最初にざっと英文に目を通し、2 回目には英文の内容を深く考えながら読み進め（その際にはメモを取りながら読んでみると良いでしょう）読み終わったら自分の言葉で英文を要約できるか確認してみましょう。3 回目には音読してみると良いでしょう。

　学習者の皆さんが各ユニットのトピックに触発されて英語へ興味を持ち、ひいては英語力向上をめざしていただけることを切に願っております。

Jonathan Lynch
Atsuko Yamamoto
Kanako Watanabe

Table of Contents

Shop Names

Pre-Reading Questions

1 What do you think is the best shop name in Japan?

2 Do you know the origin or meaning of that name?

⁰¹ Vocabulary Task ▷ 英単語とその日本語の意味を結び付けましょう。

1. product （　） a. 衣類
2. discover （　） b. 古代の
3. unique （　） c. 産物
4. clothing （　） d. 特有の
5. shorten （　） e. 発見する
6. ancient （　） f. 短くする
7. lively （　） g. 陽気な・元気な
8. well-known （　） h. 有名な・よく知られた

上記の語（句）を本文中から見つけて○をつけましょう。

⁰² Reading

NOTES

❶ When foreign people come to Japan, <u>they</u> are happy to find many nice shops. They enjoy shopping here and are pleased with both the products and the service.

❷ One more thing that <u>they</u> enjoy is discovering interesting shop names. Many shop names in Japan are written in **the Roman**

the Roman
alphabet
ローマ字

alphabet. Some examples are Uniqlo, Kaldi, Shibuya109, Doutor, United Arrows and Aeon.

❸ The names are interesting, but what do they mean? Let's check three.

🎧03 ❹ Uniqlo is an easy one. The first shop opened in Hiroshima in 1984. At that time <u>it</u> was called "Unique Clothing **Warehouse**"— a good name but too long. The company shortened <u>it</u> to "Uni-Clo" and then changed the "C" to "q". The Uniqlo **brand** was born!

warehouse 倉庫

brand 商標

❺ Kaldi Coffee Farm is another popular chain of shops in Japan. It sells coffee beans and also **imported** food products. But what does Kaldi mean? In fact, this name comes from an ancient **legend** about coffee. Long, long ago, there was a **goatherd** named Kaldi <u>who</u> lived in **Ethiopia**. One day, one of his **goats** ate some red **berries** and became very lively. Coffee beans had been discovered and now the name is famous in Japan.

imported
輸入された
legend 伝説
goatherd
ヤギ飼い
Ethiopia
エチオピア（東アフ
リカに位置する連邦
共和国）
goats （goat の複
数形）ヤギ
berries
（berry の複数形）実
origin 起源
run by
〜に経営されて

🎧04 ❻ Shibuya109 is a well-known fashion shop in Tokyo. It is open from 10:00am to 9:00pm, but that does not seem to be the **origin** of the name. Shibuya109 is **run by** the Tōkyū Group. If we change the characters of Tōkyū to numbers with the same sound, "tō" is ten and "kyū" is nine. Thus we get 109.

❼ It is fun and easy to find the meaning of shop names. Just use the Internet!

(267 words)

 **Pair Work**　下線部が何を指しているかパートナーと一緒に考えましょう。

True or False ▶ 本文の内容と一致すれば **T** (True) を、一致しなければ **F** (False) を記入しましょう。

( ) 1. Foreign people like the shops in Japan.
( ) 2. Very few shop names are written in the Roman alphabet.
( ) 3. Uniqlo's name comes from the name "United Clothing Warehouse".
( ) 4. The letter "q" in Uniqlo was originally "C".
( ) 5. Kaldi is actually the name of an animal.
( ) 6. The legend of Kaldi comes from Europe.
( ) 7. Shibuya109's name comes from the opening hours.
( ) 8. We can find the meaning of a shop name on the Internet.

Collocation

日本語をヒントに空欄を埋め意味の通る英文にしましょう。

1. The teacher was pleased （   ） the students' test results. （〜に喜ぶ）
2. Both the style （   ） the quality of this jacket are good. （〜と〜の両方とも）
3. Her first name is written （   ） hiragana. （〜で表記されて）
4. My family name comes （   ） Scotland. （〜に由来する）
5. Our shop is closed （   ） December 31st （   ） January 2nd. （〜から〜まで）

Vocabulary Quiz

空欄に ☐ の語（句）を入れて、和文と同じ意味の英文にしましょう。

ancient	clothing	discovered	lively
products	shorten	unique	well-known

1. When winter comes, the days （   ）.
   冬が来れば、日は短くなる。
2. She likes to wear dark （   ）.
   彼女は暗い色の服を着たがる。
3. Our store sells fresh farm （   ）.
   当店は新鮮な農産物を売っています。
4. Rome has many （   ） buildings.
   ローマにはたくさんの古代の建築物がある。
5. This is a （   ） party.
   これは活気のあるパーティだ。
6. Everyone has a （   ） personality.
   誰もがその人固有の性格を持っている。
7. Her name is （   ） worldwide.
   彼女の名前は世界中でよく知られている。
8. Columbus （   ） America.
   コロンブスがアメリカを発見した。

Reading Summary

下記の日本語をヒントにして空欄に当てはまる語（1語とは限りません）を入れ、本文の要約を完成させましょう。必要なら辞書を使いましょう。

Japan is （   ） its great shops. When foreign people come to Japan, they love to go shopping. However, they may wonder about the meaning of shop names. Some names are easy to explain. Uniqlo, for example, （   ） the original name of the shop... Unique Clothing Warehouse. The famous shop Kaldi, on the other hand, takes its name from a

（　　　　　　　　　　　）. Kaldi was a man who （　　　　　　　　　）goats. One of his goats ate red berries from a coffee tree and became （　　　　　　　　　）. This helped Kaldi to （　　　　　　　　　）coffee beans. Shibuya109, on the other hand, has a more modern （　　　　　　　　　）. It takes its name from the company that （　　　　　　　　）it.

| 起源 | 経営する | 元気な | 伝説 | 発見する |
| 面倒をみた | ～で有名な | ～に由来する | | |

Grammar Point + Grammar Exercise

受動態の作り方

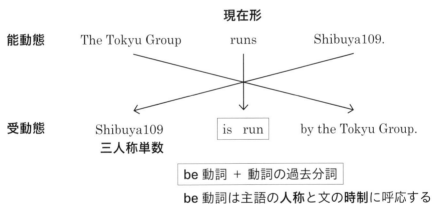

現在形

能動態　　The Tokyu Group　　runs　　Shibuya109.

受動態　　Shibuya109　　is　run　　by the Tokyu Group.
三人称単数

be 動詞 + 動詞の過去分詞
be 動詞は主語の**人称**と文の**時制**に呼応する

㋑　At that time it was called "Unique Clothing Warehouse"—a good name but too long.
Coffee beans had been discovered.

次の英文を受動態にしましょう。

1. Many people use English.
2. Natsume Soseki wrote 'Bocchan'.
3. Everybody knows Donald Trump.
4. Students must do homework.
5. My father is cooking dinner in the kitchen.

Unit 2 How to Get a Seat on a Train

Pre-Reading Questions

1 When you go somewhere by train, can you usually get a seat?

2 If you have to stand up on the train, what do you do?

☐ Try my best to get a free seat.
☐ If a seat becomes free nearby, I will take it.
☐ Nothing. I do not mind standing up.

(05) Vocabulary Task ▷ 英単語とその日本語の意味を結び付けましょう。

1. familiar ( )   a. 意図
2. tiring ( )   b. 熟練した・専門の
3. increase ( )   c. 乗客
4. expert ( )   d. 地域
5. area ( )   e. 疲れさせる
6. passenger ( )   f. 方法・戦略
7. strategy ( )   g. 増やす
8. intention ( )   h. 見慣れている・なじみのある

上記の語を本文中から見つけて○をつけましょう。

(06) Reading

❶ It is a familiar situation. You catch a train during a busy time, but there are no empty seats. If your **journey** is long, it is tiring to stand **all the way** to your **destination**.

NOTES

journey
行程（通勤・通学）
all the way
はるばる
destination　目的地

❷ How can we increase our chances of getting a seat on a crowded train?

❸ We asked some expert **commuters** in the Tokyo area for <u>their</u> best ideas on getting a seat quickly.

commuter
通勤（通学）者

⟨07⟩ **❹** The first strategy is to look for school children who are sitting down. Generally, school children do not travel far on the train. If you stand in front of <u>them</u>, <u>they</u> will probably get off after just a few stops and then you can sit down.

❺ Another good idea is to carefully choose where to stand. If you stand directly in front of a person sitting down, you have only one chance of getting a seat. However, if you **position yourself** between two seated people, you can **double** your chances. Just be careful not to **irritate** other standing passengers with this strategy.

position oneself
位置を定める
double 倍にする
irritate
いらいらさせる

⟨08⟩ **❻** One more important thing is to observe people <u>who</u> are sitting down. If you catch the same train every day, then you might see the same people sitting down every day. You can start to remember where <u>they</u> get off. Also, by observing people carefully, you can get a **hint** about <u>their</u> intentions. For example, if someone puts away a book <u>that</u> <u>they</u> are reading, <u>they</u> might get off the train soon.

hint
かすかな兆候

❼ Do you have any more ideas for getting a seat on a crowded train?

(261 words)

 **Pair Work** 下線部が何を指しているかパートナーと一緒に考えましょう。

True or False ➤ 本文の内容と一致すれば **T** (True) を、一致しなければ **F** (False) を記入しましょう。

( ) 1．People who take trains in Tokyo gave some advice for this story.
( ) 2．One idea is to talk with school children.
( ) 3．School children tend to have longer journeys.
( ) 4．Standing in front of one person is best.
( ) 5．Standing between two seated people increases your chances.
( ) 6．Looking at people's actions is important.
( ) 7．Try to remember people's routines.
( ) 8．Somebody reading a book will surely get off soon.

Collocation

日本語をヒントに空欄を埋め意味の通る英文にしましょう。

1. Do you (　　　　) a train every morning?（電車に飛び乗る）
2. The <u>chances</u> (　　　　) sunny weather this week are low.（〜の見込み）
3. The convenience store <u>is</u> (　　　) <u>front of</u> the train station.（〜の前に）
4. She goes to bed (　　　　) <u>the same time</u> every evening.（同じ時間に）
5. My younger brother never <u>puts</u> his things (　　　　).（片づける、しまう）

Vocabulary Quiz

空欄に ⬚ の語を入れて、和文と同じ意味の英文にしましょう。

area	expert	familiar	increase
intention	passengers	strategy	tiring

1. He is an (　　　　　　　　　) on the history of Japan.
   彼は日本史の専門家だ。
2. The car has seats for four (　　　　　　　).
   その車は4人分の座席がある。
3. He went to college with the (　　　　　　　) of getting special skills.
   彼は特殊技能を得るつもりで大学に行った。
4. What is your (　　　　　　　　　) for becoming a good English speaker?
   よい英語の話者になるためのあなたの戦略は何ですか。
5. People enjoyed listening to the (　　　　　　　) song.
   人々は馴染みのある歌を聞いて楽しんだ。
6. He loves his job, but he thinks it is (　　　　　　　).
   彼は自分の仕事は好きだが、それは骨が折れると思っている。
7. That (　　　　　) of the country has a lot of mountains.
   その国のその地域には多くの山がある。
8. Japan will not (　　　　　　　　) its population in the future.
   日本は今後これ以上人口を増やさないだろう。

Reading Summary

下記の日本語をヒントにして空欄に当てはまる語（1語とは限りません）を入れ、本文の要約を完成させましょう。必要なら辞書を使いましょう。

Trains are often (　　　　　　　　) and all the seats are occupied. In this situation, how can we try to (　　　　　　　) as soon as possible? There are various (　　　　　　　) that we can try. If there are school children sitting on the train, one good approach is to stand near them. In general, school children do not travel long distances, so a seat may soon become available. One more idea

is to stand（ 　　　　　　　 ）two seats rather than（ 　　　　　　　 ）
one seat. By doing this, we can（ 　　　　　　　 ）our chances of
getting a seat when somebody stands up. And of course, observing people's
（ 　　　　　　　 ）is important too. If a seated person seems to be preparing
to（ 　　　　　　　 ）the train, we can stand near them and hope to get the
vacated seat.

～の間に	降りる	行動	混んでいる
席を取る	倍にするに	方法	～の前に

Unit 2

Grammar Point + Grammar Exercise

接続詞 If の使い方
もしも～ならば

if 節の中には主語と動詞が必要です。

例 If your journey is long, it is tiring to stand all the way to your destination.

if 節の中では現在形で未来時制の代用をします。

例 If you stand in front of them, they will probably get off after just a few
stops.

If 節を主文の後に置くこともできます。この場合カンマ (,) は必要ありません。

例 You can double your chances if you position yourself between two seated
people.

日本語を参考にして英文を完成させましょう。

1．（ 　　　　　　　 ）rainy tomorrow, let's stay home.
　　もし明日雨なら、家にいましょう。

2．（ 　　　　　　　 ）this necklace, I'll give it to you.
　　もしこのネックレスが好きなら、あなたにあげます。

3．You will pass the exam easily（ 　　　　　　　　　　　　　 ）.
　　もし英語を話すことができるなら、あなたは簡単にその試験に合格するでしょう。

4．I'll order black tea for you（ 　　　　　　　　　　　 ）.
　　もしコーヒーが飲めないなら、紅茶を注文してあげます。

5．I will call you this evening（ 　　　　　　　　　　　 ）.
　　もし質問があれば今晩電話します。

Unit 3

False Rumors and Panic Buying

Pre-Reading Questions

1 Have you ever read a false rumor on the Internet or in an SNS message?

2 Why do some people start false rumors, do you think?

🎧⁽⁰⁹⁾ Vocabulary Task ▶ 英単語とその日本語の意味を結び付けましょう。

1. distribute	( )	a.	供給する、配る
2. positive	( )	b.	建設的な
3. aspect	( )	c.	すぐに
4. immediately	( )	d.	側面
5. nevertheless	( )	e.	それにもかかわらず
6. disease	( )	f.	配達
7. delivery	( )	g.	病気
8. revenge	( )	h.	報復

上記の語を本文中から見つけて○をつけましょう。

🎧⁽¹⁰⁾ Reading

❶ These days it is easy to distribute information quickly online. For important news, shopping information, entertainment and so on, <u>this</u> is a very positive aspect of the Internet.

❷ However, some people use the Internet in a bad way. Rather than **post** useful messages, they **spread false information** and

post 投稿する
spread 拡散する
false information
偽情報

false rumors.

⑪ ❸ Most Internet users are smart and can spot such **misinformation** immediately. And, to be honest, sometimes such stories can be funny.

❹ Nevertheless, false rumors can lead to big problems at times of crisis, for example, when an earthquake happens or when there is an outbreak of a **pandemic** disease.

❺ At such times, people feel nervous and want new information quickly. All kinds of rumors start to **circulate** on the Internet, especially on SNS and messaging **apps**.

⑫ ❻ One example of <u>this</u> happened during the 2020 **coronavirus** pandemic. Somebody started a rumor in Japan that toilet paper deliveries from China would stop. There was **panic buying** and soon toilet paper was **sold out** in many supermarkets.

❼ Why do people spread false rumors on the Internet?

❽ Perhaps in some cases it is a joke <u>that</u> gets out of hand. People do not understand the power of the Internet and the joke **goes too far**. In other cases, perhaps the person feels **mistreated** by society for some reasons. Thus the **false** rumor is a way to get revenge.

(225 words)

false rumor	デマ
rumor	噂
misinformation	誤報
pandemic	世界的に広がる
circulate	流布する
apps	（app の複数形、application の短縮形）アプリ、OS 上のソフトウェア
coronavirus	2019 年に中国武漢で発生したコロナウイルス
panic buying	買占め
sold out	売り切れて
go too far	行き過ぎる
mistreated	不当な扱いを受けた
false	偽りの

Unit 3

 Pair Work　下線部が何を指しているかパートナーと一緒に考えましょう。

True or False
本文の内容と一致すれば **T** (True) を、一致しなければ **F** (False) を記入しましょう。

(　) 1．Getting shopping information is a good aspect of the Internet.
(　) 2．Some people use the Internet for negative purposes.
(　) 3．It is impossible to spot misinformation.
(　) 4．False rumors stop when a crisis happens.
(　) 5．People use SNS to spread rumors.
(　) 6．Toilet paper sold out because of a false rumor.
(　) 7．False rumors are sometimes spread as a joke.
(　) 8．People spread false rumors to get revenge on a family member.

Collocation

日本語をヒントに空欄を埋め意味の通る英文にしましょう。

1. Please do not behave (   ) a bad way during the school trip.（行儀悪く）
2. (   ) than dieting, exercising is the best way to get healthy.（〜よりむしろ）
3. (   ) be honest, I did not enjoy the concert.（正直に言うと）
4. Gossiping can lead (   ) trouble.（〜という結果につながる）
5. The party was too wild and things got out of (   ).（収拾がつかなくなる）

Vocabulary Quiz

空欄に [   ] の語を入れて、和文と同じ意味の英文にしましょう。

aspect	delivery	disease	distributed
immediately	nevertheless	positive	revenge

1. She hit him out of (   ).
   彼女は仕返しで彼を叩いた。

2. He suffered from a (   ) caused by bacteria.
   彼は細菌が引き起こす病気を患った。

3. The teacher (   ) a sheet of paper to each student.
   その教師はそれぞれの生徒に1枚の紙を配布した。

4. All my efforts brought (   ) results.
   私のすべての努力はよい結果をもたらした。

5. The supermarket offers free (   ) to its customers.
   そのスーパーは顧客に無料配送を提供している。

6. One interesting (   ) of space travel was written in the book.
   宇宙旅行の興味深い一面がその本に書かれている。

7. He was sick; (   ), he didn't miss the class.
   彼は病気だが、それにもかかわらず、授業を欠席しなかった。

8. Leave here (   ), or you will miss your flight.
   直ちにここを出発しなさい、そうしなければ、あなたの乗る飛行機に乗れませんよ。

Reading Summary

下記の日本語をヒントにして空欄に当てはまる語（1語とは限りません）を入れ、本文の要約を完成させましょう。必要なら辞書を使いましょう。

The Internet is a very useful tool for spreading important information in a short time. (　　　　　　　　), not everybody uses it (　　　　　　　　). Some people spread false rumors online. (　　　　　　　　), most people are clever and are not deceived by the false information. But when a crisis (　　　　　　　　), people can get in a panic and this is the time when a lot of false rumors start to circulate online. SNS are a popular (　　　　　　　　) for spreading such rumors. A (　　　　　　　　) example occurred during the 2020 pandemic. A false rumor led to (　　　　　　　　) of toilet paper. As a result, it became (　　　　　　　　) in many shops. People may spread these false rumors as a joke or, in some cases, they may have a grudge against society.

売り切れた	起こる	買占め	幸いなことに
しかし	適切に	方法	有名な

Grammar Point + Grammar Exercise

形容詞から派生した副詞
形容詞に -ly をつける

例　These days it is easy to distribute information **quickly** online.

simple　→　simply
true　　→　truly
full　　→　fully
happy　→　happily

-ly で終わる副詞を使用して英文を完成させましょう。

1. The bad rumor spread (　　　　　　　　). （急速に）
2. The table was (　　　　　　　　) decorated with flowers. （美しく）
3. (　　　　　　　　), I could find my lost key. （幸いにも）
4. Could you speak more (　　　　　　　　)? （ゆっくりと）
5. He read the manual (　　　　　　　　) but couldn't operate the machine well. （注意深く）

Unit 4

Keeping Your Smartphone Clean

Pre-Reading Questions

1 Do you often clean your smartphone?

2 What is the best item to use to clean a smartphone, do you think?

⑬ Vocabulary Task ▷ 英単語とその日本語の意味を結び付けましょう。

1. device	( )	a. 移す
2. survey	( )	b. 化学製品
3. despite	( )	c. 装置
4. normal	( )	d. 調査
5. transfer	( )	e. ～にもかかわらず
6. item	( )	f. 標準の
7. chemical	( )	g. 品目
8. method	( )	h. 方法

上記の語を本文中から見つけて○をつけましょう。

⑭ Reading

NOTES

❶ A smartphone is a device we use many times every day. One survey reported that, on average, people check their smartphones more than 100 times per day, <u>which</u> also means that we touch <u>them</u> a lot.

❷ Despite holding and touching them so often, how many people

18

regularly clean their smartphones?

③ If truth be told, perhaps very few people do so.

④ In a normal day, we touch many surfaces, such as hanging straps on the train or door handles in public places. Our hands then transfer **bacteria** and even **viruses** from <u>these</u> surfaces to our smartphones.

⑤ Although we know we should clean our mobile devices, it is troublesome to do so. Also, people worry about using an item such as a **wet tissue** to clean the phone. Chemicals in the tissue might damage the screen or the camera lens.

⑥ Recently, a new way to clean smartphones is becoming popular. This method uses **UV light** to kill bacteria and viruses.

⑦ One type of UV light breaks down the **DNA** in **germs** and kills them. However, this light can hurt our eyes, so manufacturers have made special boxes. You put your phone inside the box, press a button and wait for 10 minutes. During that time, the UV light inside will kill almost all of the bacteria, and of course it will not damage the phone.

⑧ UV **sanitizer** boxes are convenient, **hygienic** and not so expensive. In addition, you can use <u>them</u> to **disinfect** any small item, not only smartphones.

(247 words)

bacteria
(bacterium の複数
形) 細菌
viruses
(virus の複数形)
ウイルス
wet tissue
ウェットティッシュ

UV light 紫外光

DNA
デオキシリボ核酸
germs
(germ の複数形)
病原菌

sanitizer 消毒薬
hygienic
衛生的な
disinfect
消毒する

 **Pair Work** 下線部が何を指しているかパートナーと一緒に考えましょう。

True or False

本文の内容と一致すれば **T** (True) を、一致しなければ **F** (False) を記入しましょう。

( ) 1. On average, people clean their smartphones 100 times a day.
( ) 2. In fact, most people clean their smartphones regularly.
( ) 3. Bacteria are found on surfaces in public places.
( ) 4. Our hands transfer bacteria to our phones.
( ) 5. Wet tissues are the best way to clean phones.
( ) 6. UV light can kill bacteria.
( ) 7. Put your phone in the UV box for at least one hour.
( ) 8. Unfortunately, UV sanitizer boxes cost a lot of money.

Collocation

日本語をヒントに空欄を埋め意味の通る英文にしましょう。

1. (　　　) average, we have eight rainy days a month in this season. （平均して）
2. I like amusement parks, (　　　　) (　　　　　) Disneyland and Universal Studios. （〜のような）
3. My parents worry (　　　　　　) my future, but I do not. （〜について心配する）
4. CFCs break (　　　　) ozone in the atmosphere. （破壊する）
5. (　　　) addition, this hotel room has a good view. （加えて）

Vocabulary Quiz

空欄に [　　] の語を入れて、和文と同じ意味の英文にしましょう。

device	survey	despite	normal
transferred	items	chemicals	method

1. This cleaner has dangerous (　　　　　　).
   この洗剤は危険な化学物質を含んでいる。
2. His weight is not (　　　　　　) for his age.
   彼の体重は年齢の割に標準的ではない。
3. I went hiking (　　　　　　) the bad weather.
   私は悪天候にもかかわらずハイキングに行った。
4. The smartphone is a (　　　　　　) that has changed the way we live.
   スマートフォンは私たちの生活様式を変えた装置だ。
5. Our money was (　　　　　　) to a new bank when we moved.
   私たちのお金は引っ越した時に新しい銀行に移動された。
6. She has her own (　　　　　　) of studying.
   彼女には彼女独自の勉強の仕方がある。
7. Don't forget to buy these (　　　　　　) at the supermarket.
   スーパーでこれらの品を買うのを忘れないでください。
8. They took a (　　　　　　) to get opinions about the system.
   彼らはそのシステムについての意見を得るために調査した。

Reading Summary

下記の日本語をヒントにして空欄に当てはまる語（1語とは限りません）を入れ、本文の要約を完成させましょう。必要なら辞書を使いましょう。

We (　　　　　　　　) look at and touch our smartphones many times each day. (　　　　　　　　), it seems likely that few people regularly clean their smartphones. (　　　　　　　　), bacteria and even viruses may accumulate on our phones. That surely is unhygienic and we might even become sick from the germs. People (　　　　　　　　　　) to use items such as wet tissues to clean their phones. They think that there might be harsh (　　　　　　　　) in the tissues that could damage the phone. Manufacturers have invented useful (　　　　　　　　) that can (　　　　　　　　) smartphones safely. These are small boxes and inside are UV lights. We can put a smartphone inside, press a button and leave it for a few minutes. The UV light destroys the DNA in bacteria and kills them. These UV sanitizers are (　　　　　　　　) and do not cost much.

化学製品	加えて	～する傾向にある	結果として
消毒する	装置	ためらう	便利な

Grammar Point + Grammar Exercise

although, but, however, despite の使い方
対立する内容を結び付ける

例 **Although** we know we should clean our mobile devices, it is troublesome to do so.

We know we should clean our mobile devices, **but** it is troublesome to do so.

One type of UV light breaks down the DNA in germs and kills them. **However**, this light can hurt our eyes.

Despite holding and touching them so often, how many people regularly clean their smartphones?

空欄に although, but, however, despite のいずれかを入れて意味の通る英文にしましょう。

1. He went out (　　　　　　) the bad weather.
2. (　　　　　　) the weather was bad, he went out.
3. The weather was bad; (　　　　　　), he went out.
4. The weather was bad, (　　　　　　) he went out.
5. He went out (　　　　　　) the weather was bad.

Staying Safe While Walking

Pre-Reading Questions

1 Do you ever walk and look at your smartphone at the same time?

2 Has anyone ever bumped into you while walking?

⑰ Vocabulary Task ▷ 英単語とその日本語の意味を結び付けましょう。

1. crime	( )	a. 気づいて
2. suspect	( )	b. 傲慢な
3. arrest	( )	c. 避ける
4. mentality	( )	d. 精神性
5. arrogant	( )	e. 逮捕する
6. aware	( )	f. 犯罪
7. avoid	( )	g. 連絡する
8. contact	( )	h. 容疑者

上記の語を本文中から見つけて○をつけましょう。

⑱ Reading

NOTES

❶ As people say, the world is a dangerous place. Every day, just walking along streets or through train stations, we can face many dangers.

❷ Recently, there seems to be one more danger to deal with —

people who **deliberately bump into** other people.

③ Such people can be found in any country. In Japan, they are called "butsukariya". They walk along and seem to aim at other people, using their arm or shoulder to bump into someone. Needless to say, they mainly aim at people smaller than themselves.

④ This behavior is very dangerous and could even be a crime. Some videos of people doing this have been **uploaded** to **social media**. In some cases, suspects have been arrested by the police.

⑤ It is hard to understand the mentality of people who do it. Perhaps they are not satisfied with their lives. They may be arrogant but also feel **powerless**. By bumping into people, they can feel that they have a little more power. Whatever the reason, there is no excuse for it.

⑥ We must make sure to protect ourselves against such behavior.

⑦ Firstly, do not look at your smartphone as you **walk along**. One man who was caught by the police said he deliberately aimed at so-called 'smartphone **zombies**' (people who use their smartphone while walking). Look up and be aware.

⑧ If someone seems to be aiming at you, avoid them. If someone hits you hard, make sure to contact the police.

(243 words)

deliberately	わざと
bump into	ぶつかる
uploaded	アップロードされた、更新された
social media	ソーシャルメディア
powerless	無力な
walk along	前へ歩く
zombies	(zombie の複数形) ゾンビ

Unit 5

 **Pair Work** 下線部が何を指しているかパートナーと一緒に考えましょう。

True or False ▶ 本文の内容と一致すれば **T** (True) を、一致しなければ **F** (False) を記入しましょう。

( ) 1. Everyday life has become safer recently.

( ) 2. Some people bump into other people on purpose.

( ) 3. They usually use their bags to bump into people.

( ) 4. Such behavior may be against the law.

( ) 5. The police might arrest people who bump into others.

( ) 6. The people who do it may feel powerless.

( ) 7. By using our smartphones, we can avoid these attacks.

( ) 8. If someone bumps into you hard, call the police.

Collocation

日本語をヒントに空欄を埋め意味の通る英文にしましょう。

1. At work, I often have to deal (＿＿＿＿＿) difficult customers. （扱う）
2. The archer aimed (＿＿＿) the target with his bow and arrow. （めがける）
3. (＿＿＿＿＿＿) to say, she found a good job after graduation. （言うまでもなく）
4. The student gave an excuse (＿＿＿＿＿) his poor attendance. （〜の言い訳）
5. The staff are satisfied (＿＿＿＿＿) the new computer system. （〜に満足して）

Vocabulary Quiz

空欄に　　の語を入れて、和文と同じ意味の英文にしましょう。

arrested	arrogant	aware	avoid
contacted	crime	mentality	suspect

1. My friend (＿＿＿＿＿＿＿＿) me about our vacation plan.
   私の友人は休暇の計画について私に連絡してきた。
2. We can't understand the (＿＿＿＿＿＿＿＿) of the person who killed many people.
   私たちはたくさんの人々を殺害する人の精神性を理解できない。
3. We are (＿＿＿＿＿＿＿) of the danger.
   私たちは危険に気付いている。
4. We tend to (＿＿＿＿＿＿) hard work.
   私たちはきつい仕事を避ける傾向にある。
5. He is a (＿＿＿＿＿＿) of the crime.
   彼はその犯罪の容疑者だ。
6. The police (＿＿＿＿＿＿) the criminal at last.
   警察はついに犯人を逮捕した。
7. Success made her (＿＿＿＿＿＿).
   成功は彼女を思い上がらせた。
8. Robbery is a (＿＿＿＿＿＿).
   窃盗は犯罪だ。

Reading Summary

下記の日本語をヒントにして空欄に当てはまる語（1語とは限りません）を入れ、本文の要約を完成させましょう。必要なら辞書を使いましょう。

Although there are many dangers, one particular danger has caught attention recently. Some people, it seems, deliberately (＿＿＿＿＿＿＿＿＿＿) other people when they are walking. This can happen on streets, in stations or anywhere that pedestrians pass by each other. The perpetrator aims his body at the victim and uses his arm or shoulder as a (　　　　　　　　　). The result can be (　　　　　　　　) for the victim and could cause a bruise or even cause them to fall over. In fact, this behavior may be a (　　　　　　　　　) and in some cases people have been (　　　　　　　) by the police. To (　　　　　　　　) becoming a victim, never use your smartphone when walking. If someone (　　　　　　　　) you, dodge them if possible. If someone actually hits you, by all means (　　　　　　　　) the police.

痛い	避ける	逮捕された	突き当たる
犯罪	武器	～を目がける	連絡する

Grammar Point + Grammar Exercise

 ## 形容詞や名詞を作る接尾辞

-able, -ible	形	capable	-ful	形	powerful
-ance, -ence	名	avoidance	-ic, -ical	形	fantastic
-ation, -tion	名	sensation	-ious, -ous	形	obvious
-ness	名	happiness	-less	形	powerless
-ty, -ity	名	mentality	-ly	形	friendly
-er, -or	名	teacher	-ish	形	selfish

（　　）の語に接尾辞を加えて意味の通る英文を完成させましょう。

1．This (act) is also the (write) of the famous book.
2．This singer is good at expressing the (lonely) and (sad) of young people.
3．Keep your children away from (danger) places, such as railway crossings.
4．Some electrical products are becoming (wire) and (cord).
5．Such a demand cannot be (accept).

Colorful Hairstyles

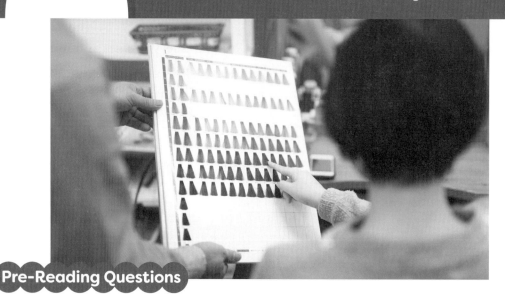

1 Have you ever dyed your hair?

2 If you dyed your hair in the near future, what color would you choose?

Vocabulary Task

英単語とその日本語の意味を結び付けましょう。

1. strict ( )   a. 薄れる・あせていく
2. trend ( )   b. 熟練者
3. option ( )   c. 勧める・推奨する
4. highlight ( )   d. 選択・選択肢
5. damaging ( )   e. 厳格な
6. professional ( )   f. 最も明るい部分
7. fade ( )   g. 流行・傾向
8. recommend ( )   h. 有害な

上記の語を本文中から見つけて○をつけましょう。

Reading

NOTES

appearance 外見

❶ Most high schools have very strict rules about **appearance**. As a result, after entering college, many young people feel a sense of freedom and want to try new fashions.

❷ Recently, one trend has been for brightly-colored hair,

sometimes called "**flashy hair**" in Japanese. Teachers at colleges in Japan have been surprised to see students with vivid pink, green, red and purple hairstyles.

③ ❸ **Besides** <u>these</u> bright colors, **pastel shades** are also popular. Some people want multi-colored hair, while others choose grey or silver coloring. Another option is to keep the natural hair color and add colorful **streaks** or highlights. For dark hair, purple or blue streaks are popular.

❹ There are two stages to getting a colorful hairstyle. Before **dyeing**, it is first necessary to **bleach** your hair. <u>This</u> process can be damaging, so it is best done by a professional **stylist**. Three **bleachings** or more may be needed.

② ❺ The second stage is coloring. <u>This</u> should also be done in a **hair salon**. The hair **colorists** there are experts and will use **the latest techniques** and high quality **dyes**.

❻ Some colorful hair dyes start to fade quickly, even after **a couple of** weeks. Special shampoos can help to keep the vivid color, and washing hair with cold water is recommended.

❼ Getting "flashy hair" is not cheap, but the final result will look fun, cute, and trendy. Would you like to try <u>it</u>?

(232 words)

---

flashy 派手な
flashy hair
派手髪

besides
〜の他にも
pastel shades
パステルカラー

streaks
(streak の複数形)
縞・線
dyeing
(dye 染める) の動名詞
bleach 脱色する
stylist = (hairstylist)
美容師
bleachings
(bleaching の複数形) 脱色
hair salon 美容院
cololorists
(colorist の複数形)
カラリスト (髪染めの技術を持つ美容師)
the latest
最新の〜
dyes
(dye 染料) の複数形
a couple of
2 (,3) の

Unit 6

 **Pair Work** 下線部が何を指しているかパートナーと一緒に考えましょう。

True or False

▶ 本文の内容と一致すれば **T** (True) を、一致しなければ **F** (False) を記入しましょう。

( ) 1. Colleges have strict rules about appearance.
( ) 2. "Flashy hair" usually means brightly colored hair.
( ) 3. Grey or silver coloring options are not available.
( ) 4. Purple streaks are popular for people with dark hair.
( ) 5. There are two steps for getting a colorful hairstyle.
( ) 6. It is best to do bleaching at home.
( ) 7. It is best to do dyeing at home.
( ) 8. Maintenance is important because vivid colors can fade fast.

Collocation

日本語をヒントに空欄を埋め意味の通る英文にしましょう。

1. A typhoon hit last weekend. As a (＿＿＿＿＿＿＿＿), our barbecue was cancelled.

（その結果）

2. Traveling gives me a sense (＿＿＿) freedom. （解放感）
3. In America, we often see people (＿＿＿＿＿) tattoos. （〜を持った）
4. There are four stages (＿＿＿) baking bread. （〜への段階）
5. I have been waiting for my friend for (＿＿＿) (＿＿＿) (＿＿＿) hours. （2、3の）

Vocabulary Quiz

空欄に ⬚⬚⬚ の語を入れて、和文と同じ意味の英文にしましょう。

damaging	faded	highlights	option
professional	recommend	strict	trend

1. For losing weight, I (＿＿＿＿＿＿＿＿＿) swimming.
   減量には水泳をお勧めします。

2. The color of the picture taken decades ago has (＿＿＿＿＿).
   何十年も前に撮られた写真は色あせてしまった。

3. His mother is very (＿＿＿＿＿) about manners.
   彼の母親はマナーにとても厳しい。

4. She is a (＿＿＿＿＿＿) nail artist, so she always does a good job.
   彼女はプロのネイルアーティストなので、いつも良い仕事をする。

5. Shorter hairstyles are the new (＿＿＿＿＿＿＿) for this season.
   ショートヘアは今シーズンの新しい傾向だ。

6. Too much sunlight is (＿＿＿＿＿＿) for your skin.
   太陽の光に当たりすぎると肌に悪い。

7. Which (＿＿＿＿＿＿＿) do you prefer? Permed hair or straight hair?
   どちらの選択肢が好みですか。パーマをかけた髪ですか、それともストレートですか。

8. I am planning to get light-brown (＿＿＿＿＿＿＿＿) for my hair.
   私は髪に明るい茶色のハイライトを入れるつもりです。

Reading Summary

下記の日本語をヒントにして空欄に当てはまる語（1語とは限りません）を入れ、本文の要約を完成させましょう。必要なら辞書を使いましょう。

Young people at colleges in Japan like to experiment with new fashions. The time between high school and entering a company might be their only chance to try a brightly-colored hairstyle. Vivid colors such as red or green are popular, but there are also other (＿＿＿＿＿＿＿＿＿＿). Some of the more subtle* choices include pastel shades, colorful streaks or colorful (   ). For Japanese people who have naturally dark hair, adding (   ) of blue or purple might be popular. Getting so-called "flashy hair" involves two processes: first (   ) the hair and then (   ) the hair. Each of these steps should be done at a hair salon by a (   ). Because the color may (   ), maintenance with special shampoos (   ).

*subtle　微妙な

推奨される	すぐにあせる	線	選択肢
専門家	染める	脱色する	最も明るい部分

Grammar Point + Grammar Exercise

 不定代名詞

例　**Some** people want multi-colored hair, while **others** choose grey or silver coloring. Another option is to keep the natural hair color and add colorful **streaks** or highlights.

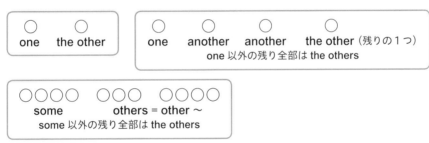

日本語を参考にして、空欄に適切な上記の語（句）を選んで入れましょう。

1. I have two DVDs. (   ) is "Star Wars," and (   ) is "The Lion King." Which do you want to watch?
   2枚の DVD があります。1枚はスターウォーズで、もう1枚はライオンキングです。どちらを観たいですか。

2. This shirt is nice. But could you show me (   ) color?
   このシャツはいいですね。でも、別の色を見せてください。

3. I'm a member of the soccer team. I'm a freshman but (   ) are second year students.　僕はサッカー部の一員です。僕は1年生ですが、他は2年生です。

4. (   ) students like math, and (   ) like science in this class.
   このクラスには数学が好きな学生もいれば、科学が好きな学生もいます。

5. I met three people yesterday. One was Chinese, another was Russian and (   ) was Mexican.
   昨日、3人の人たちに会いました。1人は中国人で、もう1人はロシア人、残りの1人はメキシコ人でした。

Smartphone Cameras

Pre-Reading Questions

1 Do you often take photos on your smartphone?

2 Which is your **best** recent smartphone photo? Check your smartphone photos now. Choose your **best recent photo**. Show it to your classmates and teacher.

(25) Vocabulary Task ▷ 英単語とその日本語の意味を結び付けましょう。

1. original	( )	a. 押しボタン
2. minor	( )	b. 解決する
3. feature	( )	c. 結合する
4. button	( )	d. 最初の
5. compose	( )	e. 優れた
6. solve	( )	f. 作る
7. combine	( )	g. 特徴
8. excellent	( )	h. 目立たない・比較的重要でない

上記の語を本文中から見つけて○をつけましょう。

(26) Reading

❶ When **Steve Jobs** announced the first **iPhone** in 2007, he introduced it as a device that combined three things: a **mobile**

NOTES

Steve Jobs
アメリカの実業家、
アップル社の共同設
立者

phone, an **iPod portable media player**, and an **Internet browser**.

❷ The original iPhone had a camera of course, but <u>it</u> only seemed to be a minor feature of the device.

⑵₇ ❸ These days, things have changed. When people get a new iPhone or any smartphone, what <u>they</u> want most is a really good camera.

❹ The good news is that smartphone cameras are now, in fact, the best cameras. There are several reasons for <u>this</u>.

❺ First, think of the way we take photos with a smartphone. We do not look through a **viewfinder** and press buttons — we just look at the big screen and touch it to take a shot. We can easily compose wonderful photos in <u>this</u> way.

⑵₈ ❻ Second, the lenses. In the past, <u>these</u> were a problem for smartphones. A bigger lens takes better pictures, but smartphone lenses are tiny. Fortunately, <u>this</u> has now been solved. The latest smartphones have two or even three lenses. Data is combined from the lenses to make beautiful pictures.

❼ Third, smartphone camera **apps** are excellent. <u>They</u> make it super easy to take and share nice pictures.

❽ But the best thing about a smartphone camera is that <u>it</u> is always in your pocket. A big camera will often be left at home. As people say, the best camera is the one you have with you. (236 words)

Pair Work　下線部が何を指しているかパートナーと一緒に考えましょう。

True or False

本文の内容と一致すれば **T** (True) を、一致しなければ **F** (False) を記入しましょう。

( ) 1. The original iPhone appeared more than 10 years ago.
( ) 2. Steve Jobs said that it had three main functions.
( ) 3. The original iPhone did not have a camera.
( ) 4. People now want excellent cameras in their smartphones.
( ) 5. The big smartphone screen is good for taking pictures.
( ) 6. These days, lenses are a weak point of smartphone cameras.
( ) 7. The latest smartphones have multiple lenses.
( ) 8. People tend to leave their smartphones at home.

Collocation

日本語をヒントに空欄を埋め意味の通る英文にしましょう。

1. We don't know <u>the reasons</u> (   ) our computer problems. （～の理由）
2. <u>Look</u> (   ) this telescope. You can see Jupiter! （～をのぞく）
3. I want to (   ) <u>a shot</u> of this wonderful view. （写真を撮る）
4. (   ) this way, we can easily learn a new language. （このように）
5. (   ) the past, people read more books. （過去に）

Vocabulary Quiz

空欄に ⬚⬚ の語を入れて、和文と同じ意味の英文にしましょう。

| button | combine | compose | excellent |
| feature | minor | original | solving |

1. The biggest (   ) of the prefecture is a lake.
   その県の最大の特徴は湖です。
2. A (   ) error can lead to a serious incident.
   小さな誤りが重大な事故につながることがある。
3. Push this (   ) to switch on the projector.
   このボタンを押してプロジェクターのスイッチを入れてください。
4. Move your position to (   ) a good photo.
   良い写真を撮るために位置を移動してください。
5. My younger sister is good at (   ) math problems.
   妹は数学の問題を解くのが得意だ。
6. This yoga event will (   ) both fun and fitness.
   このヨガのイベントは楽しみと健康の両方を結び付ける。
7. New Amsterdam was the (   ) name of New York City.
   ニューアムステルダムはニューヨークシティの元の名前だった。
8. The students are (   ). They always study hard.
   その学生たちは優秀だ。彼らはいつも熱心に勉強する。

Reading Summary ▷

下記の日本語をヒントにして空欄に当てはまる語（1語とは限りません）を入れ、本文の要約を完成させましょう。必要なら辞書を使いましょう。

Smartphones have existed for quite a long time. (　　　　　　　) they were mainly viewed as mobile phones, media players and Internet browsing (　　　　　　　). However, over time, the cameras on smartphones have become more and more important to users. (　　　　　　　), these days, when people buy a new smartphone, the number one (　　　　　　　) is the camera. Smartphone cameras are the best cameras (　　　　　　　). First, the big screen makes it simple to (　　　　　　　) a great photo. Second, the latest cameras have several lenses. The smartphone automatically merges the data from each lens to give beautiful pictures. (　　　　　　　), smartphone camera apps are very (　　　　　　　) and finally we always have our smartphone with us. That means we never miss a shot.

いくつかの理由で	加えて	実際のところ	装置
作る	特徴	初めは	便利な

Grammar Point + Grammar Exercise

 ## make A B 「A を B にする」

例 Smartphone cameras **make it super easy** to take and share nice pictures.

B には補語（名詞、形容詞、現在分詞、過去分詞）が入ります。また、make の他に keep (keep A B で「A を B に保つ」) や leave(leave A B で「A を B にしておく」) でも同様の使い方をします。

make her happy（彼女を幸せにする）
make it easy to cook steak（ステーキを調理することを簡単にする）it = to cook steak

次の文を日本語に訳しましょう。
1. What made you so surprised?
2. They will make their son a politician against his will.
3. His explanation made the problem more difficult.
4. Keep your room clean, or I'll throw away all of your toys.
5. Don't leave the door open.

Unit 8 Smartwatches

Pre-Reading Questions

1 Are you wearing a watch today?

2 If yes, why did you choose that style of watch? If no, why not?

⁽²⁹⁾ Vocabulary Task ▶ 英単語とその日本語の意味を結び付けましょう。

1. gradually （　） a. 次第に
2. convenience （　） b. 返答する
3. connect （　） c. 探知する・追跡する
4. reply （　） d. つながる
5. schedule （　） e. 特に
6. replace （　） f. 取り替える
7. especially （　） g. 便利（なこと）
8. track （　） h. 予定

上記の語を本文中から見つけて○をつけましょう。

⁽³⁰⁾ Reading

NOTES

❶ Do you know anybody <u>who</u> wears a smartwatch?

❷ It seems that few people wear <u>them</u>, but sales are gradually increasing. Maybe it is the time to ask questions such as, "Do I want a smartwatch? Do I need a smartwatch?"

3 To answer <u>these</u> questions, let's think about the advantages of having a smartwatch.

4 The first good point about smartwatches is convenience. <u>They</u> connect to your smartphone and let you do many things. You can take a call on a smartwatch, check messages, reply to messages, get schedule **reminders**, listen to music and more. You can do all <u>these</u> things without taking your smartphone out of your pocket or bag. That is very convenient.

5 Another good point is the design. Modern smartwatches look really cool, and you can change the **watch face**. If you get tired of one face, just download a new <u>one</u>. The **band** can also be replaced, so it is easy to **give your watch a makeover**.

6 Using smartwatches to pay for things or to ride a train is also very convenient. Just put your smartwatch near the **card reader** in a shop or at a ticket gate in a station. It is better than **taking out** a smartphone, especially when you are in a rush.

7 And another nice aspect is **fitness**. Smartwatches track your steps, **heartbeat**, cycling time and more. If you are planning to get **fitter**, <u>they</u> might be a very useful tool.

8 What do you think? Might you buy a smartwatch?

(247 words)

reminders
(reminder の複数形)
リマインダー（予定
などを知らせる機能）

watch face
時計の文字盤
band
時計のベルト、バンド
give ~ a makeover
~を改造、変更する
card reader
カードの情報の読み取り装置
take out 取り出す
fitness 健康

heartbeat 心拍数

fitter （fit 健康な）の比較級

Unit 8

 **Pair Work** 下線部が何を指しているかパートナーと一緒に考えましょう。

True or False

本文の内容と一致すれば **T** (True) を、一致しなければ **F** (False) を記入しましょう。

( ) 1. Not so many people have smartwatches.
( ) 2. However, more people are buying them.
( ) 3. Smartwatches can perform many functions.
( ) 4. Unfortunately, we cannot play music with a smartwatch.
( ) 5. To use a smartwatch, you must take out your smartphone.
( ) 6. Most smartwatches have a boring design.
( ) 7. We can use smartwatches for purchases.
( ) 8. Smartwatches lack fitness functions.

Collocation

日本語をヒントに空欄を埋め意味の通る英文にしましょう。

1. What are the advantages (　　　　) working from home? （〜の利点）
2. I cannot (　　　　) a call this afternoon. I will be in a meeting. （電話に出る）
3. I get tired (　　　　) the same celebrities on TV every day. （〜に飽きる）
4. Can you pay (　　　　) this meal? I forgot my wallet. （〜の支払いをする）
5. If I am (　　　　) a rush in the morning, I skip breakfast. （急いで）

Vocabulary Quiz

空欄に [____] の語を入れて、和文と同じ意味の英文にしましょう。

| connect | convenience | especially | gradually |
| replies | schedule | tracks | replace |

1. I like the (　　　　　　　) of online shopping.
   私はオンラインショッピングの利便性が好きです。

2. If you use an LED bulb, you don't have to (　　　　　　　) it so often.
   LED 電球を使えばそう頻繁に取り換える必要はない。

3. My grandmother can (　　　　　　　) her computer to the Internet.
   私の祖母はコンピュータをインターネットにつなげることができる。

4. My father never (　　　　　　　) to my emails.
   私の父は決して私のメールに返事をしません。

5. I use my smartphone calendar to organize my (　　　　　　　).
   私は予定を立てるためにスマホのカレンダーを使います。

6. This app is good for parents. It (　　　　　　　) my children's movements.
   このアプリは親にとっては良い。それは子供の移動を追跡してくれる。

7. My English is (　　　　　　　) improving.
   私の英語は徐々に上達している。

8. I love watching movies, (　　　　　　　) action movies.
   私は映画、特にアクション映画を観るのが大好きです。

Reading Summary

下記の日本語をヒントにして空欄に当てはまる語（1語とは限りません）を入れ、本文の要約を完成させましょう。必要なら辞書を使いましょう。

Smartwatches have gained attention recently, but relatively few people seem to have one. Perhaps now might be a good time to consider their (   ). Above all, smartwatches are very (   ). They (   ) to your smartphone and perform many of the same (   ). The convenience is that your smartphone can remain in your pocket or bag. That might be really useful on a crowded train for example. Smartwatches also have very nice designs. In addition, you can change your smartwatch's appearance, by downloading a new (   ) or by changing the (   ). Smartwatch users can (   ) things easily, and also use their smartwatch to ride on a train. Finally, they are (   ) fitness monitors.

機能	つながる	時計のバンド	～の支払いをする
便利な	文字盤	優秀な	利点

Grammar Point + Grammar Exercise

 few と little

例 **Few** people wear smartwatches, but sales are gradually increasing.

	たくさんの	少しの	ほとんど～ない
数えられる名詞とともに使う	many	a few	few
数えられない名詞とともに使う	much	a little	little

空欄に上記の適切な語（句）を入れましょう。

1. How (   ) salt do you put in this soup?
2. I have (   ) free time, so I cannot speak to you today.
3. I can eat steak only (   ) times a year.
4. He likes comic books and therefore has read (   ) novels.
5. There is (   ) news about the disaster. We do not know the real situation.

Have You Joined a Club or Circle?

Pre-Reading Questions

1 Are you a member of a college club or circle?

2 If yes, which one? If no, why not?

Vocabulary Task ▶ 英単語とその日本語の意味を結び付けましょう。

1. absorb ( ) a. 顕著な
2. noticeable ( ) b. 最優先事項
3. factor ( ) c. 要因
4. mention ( ) d. 吸収する、取り入れる
5. male ( ) e. 伝統、習慣
6. priority ( ) f. 負担
7. burden ( ) g. 男性の
8. tradition ( ) h. 述べる

上記の語を本文中から見つけて○をつけましょう。

Reading

NOTES

1 Entering college can be a big shock for young people. The **lifestyle** is different, there is a lot of information to absorb, and there are many new people to meet.

2 One of the first things to decide is which club or circle to join.

lifestyle
生活様式

Do you continue with the same kind of club as high school or do you try something new?

(35) **3** Recently, a new trend has become noticeable. Some new students do not join any club or circle.

4 To understand the **thinking** of these students, we spoke to several college students from Tokyo, all of whom had never joined a club or circle at college.

thinking 考え

5 One of the main factors these students mentioned was freedom. One male student, for example, said that he belonged to the **track and field** club in high school. That club was strict and activities took up a lot of his time. At college, he said, he wanted more free time for himself and also wanted to decide his **own** schedule freely.

track and field
陸上競技

~ own ～自身の

(36) **6** Another factor was part time jobs. Several students said that **doing a part time job** was a priority (second to studying, of course). They felt that doing circle activities and a part time job would be too much of a burden.

do a part time job
アルバイトをする

7 And one more factor seems to be **individuality**. More young people do not worry about **existing** customs or traditions. They want to enjoy university life in their own style.

individuality
個別性
existing
従来の

(238 words)

Unit 9

 **Pair Work** 下線部が何を指しているかパートナーと一緒に考えましょう。

True or False ▶ 本文の内容と一致すれば **T** (True) を、一致しなければ **F** (False) を記入しましょう。

( ) 1. The lifestyle in college is nearly the same as in high school.
( ) 2. Deciding a club or circle is a priority for most freshmen.
( ) 3. Clubs and circles are compulsory in many colleges.
( ) 4. College students from around the world were surveyed.
( ) 5. Some college students want freedom.
( ) 6. The male student wanted more free time at college.
( ) 7. Some students think that doing a part time job is important.
( ) 8. All students are following existing customs.

Collocation

日本語をヒントに空欄を埋め意味の通る英文にしましょう。

1. We had a sudden blackout at school, but our teacher continued (　　　　　) the class. （～を続ける）
2. I belong (　　　) a gym near my house. （属する）
3. The president's speech took (　　　) most of the ceremony. （～を占める）
4. I worry (　　　　) my son's future. （～を心配する）
5. He is a workaholic. Having fun is second (　　　) his job. （～に次いで）

Vocabulary Quiz

空欄に ⬚ の語を入れて、和文と同じ意味の英文にしましょう。

absorb	burden	factor	mentioned
male	noticeable	priority	tradition

1. The disease does not have any (　　　　　　　) symptoms in the early stages.
   その病気は初期段階では顕著な症状がない。
2. Smoking is the biggest (　　　　　) for lung cancer.
   喫煙は肺がんの最大の要因だ。
3. Wearing a yukata is a summer (　　　　　) in Japan.
   浴衣を着ることは日本の夏の伝統です。
4. It is interesting to (　　　　　) foreign cultures.
   外国の文化を取り入れるのは興味深い。
5. This job is a (　　　　　　　). Please finish it first.
   この仕事が優先です。先に仕上げてください。
6. The number of (　　　　) nurses is increasing.
   男性の看護師が増えている。
7. We changed the plan as (　　　　　) below.
   下記のように計画を変更しました。
8. The cost of education is a big (　　　　　) on many families.
   教育費は多くの家族に大きな負担になっている。

Reading Summary ▷

下記の日本語をヒントにして空欄に当てはまる語（１語とは限りません）を入れ、本文の要約を完成させましょう。必要なら辞書を使いましょう。

When they enter college, young people have to （　　　　　　　） quickly to the new （　　　　　　　）. They are busy with many things and one of these is deciding which club or circle to join. At most colleges, there is a wide range to choose from. However, recently, some students are opting to not join any club or circle. There may be some reasons to explain their （　　　　　　　）. One may be that they want more freedom. High school clubs in particular can be strict, and also （　　　　　　　） a lot of time. （　　　　　　　）, after high school, some students want to （　　　　　　　） their time freely. Another reason might be part time jobs. Doing club activities and （　　　　　　　） may be too much for some students. They might prioritize their part time job. （　　　　　　　）, modern students may be more individualistic.

*opt　選ぶ

| アルバイトをする | 過ごす | ふるまい | したがって |
| 環境 | 適応する | 占める | 最終的に |

Grammar Point + Grammar Exercise

 ## 自動詞と他動詞

目的語をとらないのが自動詞、目的語をとるのが他動詞です。

例　He **belonged** to the track and field club in high school.　→　自動詞
　　He didn't **join** any clubs in high school.　→　他動詞

下線部の動詞について自動詞か他動詞か答えましょう。

1. When my father <u>came</u> home, I was <u>listening</u> to radio.
2. I <u>spoke</u> to many people in English during my stay in London.
3. Did you <u>enjoy</u> the welcome party for the new students last night?
4. I <u>had</u> a cold but I <u>feel</u> better now.
5. She does not fully <u>understand</u> the importance of diversity.

Unit 10 Are Typhoons Becoming More Dangerous?

Pre-Reading Questions

1 What do you think of typhoons?

2 What is the worst aspect of typhoons, do you think?

(37) Vocabulary Task ▷ 英単語とその日本語の意味を結び付けましょう。

1. scary	( )	a. 深刻な
2. cause	( )	b. 自然災害
3. huge	( )	c. 〜の原因となる
4. region	( )	d. 地域
5. severe	( )	e. 巨大な
6. hit	( )	f. 恐ろしい
7. flood	( )	g. 水浸しにする
8. disaster	( )	h. 襲う

上記の語を本文中から見つけて○をつけましょう。

(38) Reading

❶ Have you thought that typhoons seem to be more dangerous these days? **Not only** more dangerous, **but** scarier, too.

❷ Recent typhoons have caused a lot of damage and sadly killed many people, too.

NOTES

not only A but (also) B
A だけでなく B も

³⁹ **3** Do you remember Typhoon **Hagibis** (Typhoon #19) in 2019? That was a huge and powerful typhoon that hit the **Kanto region** on a Saturday in October. Many people stayed at home all day. **Emergency warning messages** continuously arrived on smartphones. There were severe floods and many buildings were damaged. It was a very scary typhoon.

4 A year before that, Typhoon **Jebi** (Typhoon #21) hit the **Kansai region**. Kansai International Airport was flooded and a ship damaged the bridge connecting the airport to Osaka. Many people were **trapped** at the airport.

⁴⁰ **5** These and other typhoons have certainly been dangerous. However, when they hit Japan, they were actually weaker than their **peak**. At landfall, Jebi was category 3 (on the American scale) and Hagibis was category 2.

6 On this scale, category 5 is the strongest storm. Typhoon **Vera (the Isewan Typhoon)** was a category 5 typhoon when it hit Japan in 1959. This caused a terrible disaster, particularly in the Nagoya area. Over 5000 people died.

7 Could a **super typhoon** like Vera hit again? We must be prepared.

(210 words)

Hagibis
ハギビス（フィリピン命名。「迅速な通過」の意味）
Kanto region
関東地方
emergency warning
非常警報
emergency warning messages
「エリアメール」や「緊急速報メール」等
Jebi
チェービー（韓国命名）
Kansai region
関西地方
trapped
（trap 足止めする）の過去分詞形
peak ピーク時

Vera ヴェラ
the Isewan Typhoon
伊勢湾台風

super typhoon
スーパー台風

 Pair Work 下線部が何を指しているかパートナーと一緒に考えましょう。

True or False

▶ 本文の内容と一致すれば **T**（True）を、一致しなければ **F**（False）を記入しましょう。

(　) 1. Recent typhoons have been destructive.
(　) 2. Typhoon Hagibis hit Japan in 2019.
(　) 3. There was not much damage from Typhoon Hagibis.
(　) 4. Typhoon Jebi hit the Kansai region in 2018.
(　) 5. Narita Airport was affected by Typhoon Jebi.
(　) 6. Typhoon Jebi was the strongest ever typhoon to hit Japan.
(　) 7. The strongest typhoons are category 6 typhoons.
(　) 8. Typhoon Vera caused terrible damage in the Chubu region.

Unit 10

Collocation

> 日本語をヒントに空欄を埋め意味の通る英文にしましょう。

1. I spent ( ) day doing nothing yesterday. （一日中）
2. Playing games ( ) smartphones has become very popular. （スマホで）
3. The Akashi-Kaikyo Bridge connects Awaji Island ( ) Honshu. （～を…につなげる）
4. The hurricane was very strong ( ) landfall. （上陸時に）
5. Japan's earthquake scale is from 1 to 7. ( ) this scale, 7 is strongest.

（このスケールで）

Vocabulary Quiz

> 空欄に ▢ の語（句）を入れて、和文と同じ意味の英文にしましょう。

cause	disaster	be flooded	hit
huge	region	scary	severe

1. Smoking can ( ) lung cancer.
   喫煙は肺がんを引き起こすことがあります。

2. A powerful earthquake ( ) eastern Japan in 2011.
   2011 年、大規模な地震が東日本を襲いました。

3. The sinking of the Titanic was a ( ) that happened in 1912.
   タイタニック号の沈没は 1912 年に起きた災害でした。

4. I can hear a ( ) sound from the empty house.
   その空き家から恐ろしい音が聞こえる。

5. I have a ( ) allergy to shellfish.
   私は深刻な甲殻類アレルギーを持っています。

6. He is the captain of a ( ) tanker.
   彼は大型タンカーの船長です。

7. Areas near the river might ( ) during a typhoon.
   台風の間、川の近くの地域は浸水するかもしれない。

8. The Tohoku ( ) was hit by a large earthquake.
   東北地方は大きな地震に襲われた。

Reading Summary

下記の日本語をヒントにして空欄に当てはまる語（1 語とは限りません）を入れ、本文の要約を完成させましょう。必要なら辞書を使いましょう。

Recently it seems that typhoons have become more ( ) and ( ) than before. Violent typhoons can ( ) damage to buildings, flooding and loss of life. One example of such a typhoon was Typhoon Hagibis. It ( ) Japan in 2019 and caused a lot of damage and deaths in the Kanto (   ). Many people remember it because it happened during the Rugby World Cup and some matches (   ). People also remember the continuous emergency warning messages on their smartphones that day.

A (   ) strong typhoon hit the Kansai region in 2018. However, stronger typhoons are possible. A category 5 typhoon hit Japan over 60 years ago in the Chubu region. Many people sadly died and, of course, a similar super typhoon might strike again (   ).

襲った	危険な	将来に	地域
中止された	同様の	引き起こす	より恐ろしい

Grammar Point + Grammar Exercise

 比較級と最上級の作り方

例 They were actually **weaker than** their peak.
   Category 5 is **the strongest** storm.

	1 音節	2 音節以上	2 音節で -y, -er, -le, -ow で終わる	不規則変化
比較級	～ er	more ～	～ er	例 better
最上級	～ est	the most ～	～ est	例 best

以下の表を完成させましょう。

原級	比較級	最上級
hot		
useful		
clever		
narrow		
scary		
wise		
important		
bad		

Unit 10

45

Unit 11

Learning English Through Gaming

Pre-Reading Questions

1 Do you play games? (on a smartphone, tablet, PC, console, etc.)

2 If yes, what are your favorite games? If no, why not?

Vocabulary Task

英単語とその日本語の意味を結び付けましょう。

1. adult	( )		a. 役割
2. negative	( )		b. 大人
3. image	( )		c. 想像する
4. role	( )		d. 指示
5. improve	( )		e. 良くない
6. imagine	( )		f. 向上させる
7. skill	( )		g. 印象
8. instruction	( )		h. 技能

上記の語を本文中から見つけて○をつけましょう。

Reading

1 Some adults have a negative image of gaming and **gamers**.

2 However, one great point about games is that you can learn English while playing.

3 The best games for learning English are online games,

NOTES

gamer
コンピュータゲーム
をする人々の総称

46

sometimes called **MMO games** (massively multiplayer online games). Among <u>these</u>, **RPGs** (role playing games) may be particularly useful for improving your English. A famous example of an MMORPG is '**World of Warcraft**'.

(43) **4** So let's imagine that you start playing **WoW**. How does <u>it</u> help your English skills?

5 Firstly, you have to read instructions and information during the game. You have to make your **character** and then your character will interact with other characters. Your reading skills will start to improve immediately.

6 Players in WoW and other games make groups, called **guilds**. It is more fun to play in a guild and many guild members become **online friends**.

(44) **7** You can use **text chat** to communicate with guild members, but the best way is **voice chat**. With a headset, you can chat in real time with your guild **mates**. Isn't <u>this</u> a great way to improve your English speaking and listening skills?

8 Also, you do not have to worry about speaking 'perfect English'. MMOs are played by gamers from all over the world. Most are not **native speakers**, so nobody cares about mistakes. **After all**, the main goal is enjoying the game!

(223 words)

| MMO game |
| 大規模多人数同時参加型オンラインゲーム |
| **RPG** |
| ロールプレーイングゲーム |
| **World of Warcraft** |
| ワールドオブウォークラフト（オンラインゲーム） |
| **WoW** = World of Warcraft |
| **character** |
| ゲーム上のキャラクター |
| **guild** |
| ギルド、組合 |
| **online friend** |
| オンライン上の友達 |
| **text chat** |
| テキストチャット、文字でのやり取り |
| **voice chat** |
| ボイスチャット、音声でのやり取り |
| **mate** 仲間、友達 |
| **native speaker** |
| 母国語話者 |
| **after all** 結局 |

 **Pair Work** 下線部が何を指しているかパートナーと一緒に考えましょう。

Unit 11

True or False ▶ 本文の内容と一致すれば **T**（True）を、一致しなければ **F**（False）を記入しましょう。

( ) 1. Some adults think gaming is not good.
( ) 2. We can use games to study English.
( ) 3. 'World of Warcraft' is an online game.
( ) 4. Players read English during the game.
( ) 5. It takes a long time to improve reading ability.
( ) 6. Text chat is the best way to communicate.
( ) 7. Guild mates often meet and talk in person.
( ) 8. Most online gamers are not native speakers of English.

Collocation

日本語をヒントに空欄を埋め意味の通る英文にしましょう。

1. This app is useful (　　　　　) memorizing English words. （〜に有益な）
2. It is sometimes troublesome to interact (　　　　　) neighbors. （〜と交流する）
3. Teachers sometimes communicate (　　　　　) students by using SNS.
   （〜と意思疎通をする）。
4. During my online lesson, I can speak (　　　　) real time with my teacher.
   （リアルタイムで、実時間で）
5. She is kind and cares (　　　　　) other people. （〜を気にかける）

Vocabulary Quiz

空欄に [　　] の語を入れて、和文と同じ意味の英文にしましょう。

adults	instructions	image	imagine
improve	negative	role	skill

1. Thanks to the TV commercial, most people have a good (　　　　　) of that
   product.
   テレビ CM のおかげで、ほとんどの人がその商品に良いイメージを持っています。
2. I often (　　　　　　　) living life on a tropical island.
   私はしばしば南の島での暮らしを想像する。
3. I had a (　　　　　　　) impression of the man because of his bad language.
   ひどい言葉遣いのせいで私はその男性に良くない印象を持った。
4. What I lack is negotiation (　　　　　).
   私に足りないのは交渉の技術だ。
5. This game is suitable for both kids and (　　　　　).
   このゲームは子供にも大人にも適している。
6. We will (　　　　　) our service by listening to customers' complaints.
   顧客の苦情を聞くことで私たちのサービスを向上できるだろう。
7. Before taking this medicine, please read the attached (　　　　　　　　)
   carefully.
   この薬を飲む前に、付属の指示をよく読んでください。
8. The director gave her an important (　　　　　) in the play.
   監督は彼女にお芝居の重要な役割を与えた。

Reading Summary ▷

下記の日本語をヒントにして空欄に当てはまる語（1語とは限りません）を入れ、本文の要約を完成させましょう。必要なら辞書を使いましょう。

Although some （　　　　　　　　　　　） criticize gaming, there may be some good points about it. One point is that gamers can （　　　　　　　　　　） their English just by playing games. If you want to try it, English teachers （　　　　　　　　） online games and especially online role-playing games. One popular online RPG is World of Warcraft, which is enjoyed by millions of players around the world. Just by setting up your character and meeting other characters in the game, you will read a lot of English and improve your reading （　　　　　　　　　　）. In the game, guilds are popular. These are groups of players who work together and help （　　　　　　　　　　）. By texting your guild friends, you can improve your writing skills. Furthermore, if you buy a （　　　　　　　　） headset, you can （　　　　　　　　　） with them and enjoy gaming and learning English （　　　　　　　　）.

おしゃべりする	お互いに	大人たち	技能
向上させる	薦める	同時に	安い

Grammar Point + Grammar Exercise

 後置修飾

例 The best games for learning English are online games, sometimes **called** MMO games. → 過去分詞が後ろから前にある名詞を修飾「〜される、〜された」

Look at the cat sleeping on the sofa.
　　　　　　　　　　→ 現在分詞が後ろから前にある名詞を修飾「〜している」

分詞に注意して、次の英文を日本語にしましょう。

1. I have a car made in Germany.
2. This is the most popular dress of all designed by that designer.
3. The meat cooked over a high heat was burned.
4. Do you know the man taking photos over there?
5. The role given to me is to protect people working for other people.

Unit 11

Maroon 5

Pre-Reading Questions

1 What is your favorite type of music?

2 Who is your favorite artist?

(45) Vocabulary Task ▶ 英単語とその日本語の意味を結び付けましょう。

1. originally	( )	a. 拡大する、増える
2. expand	( )	b. 関係
3. distinctive	( )	c. 元々は
4. relationship	( )	d. 進化する
5. actually	( )	e. 独特な
6. lyric	( )	f. 歌詞
7. appear	( )	g. 実際に
8. evolve	( )	h. 現れる、登場する

上記の語を本文中から見つけて○をつけましょう。

(46) Reading

❶ Have you heard of the **band**, Maroon 5? This group from California might be the most popular band in the world.

❷ The name suggests that there are five members. Originally **there were**, but <u>it</u> has now expanded to seven.

NOTES

band バンド

there were
these were five
members の省略

3 **Adam Levine** is the band's **lead singer**. He sings with a high voice, <u>which</u> makes Maroon 5 songs distinctive. However, it also makes <u>them</u> a little difficult to sing at karaoke.

(47) **4** Maroon 5's first big **hit** was the **single** "This Love" in 2004. It is a song about a relationship <u>that</u> is ending. Actually, the lyrics are based on Adam's girlfriend at that time.

5 "This Love" appeared on Maroon 5's **debut album**, "Songs About Jane". Several more songs from this album were also hits and the album is still popular today.

6 Since 2004, Maroon 5's popularity has gone up and down. Some of their singles have been hits, while others were not so popular. However, <u>they</u> always keep going and then come back with a big hit. Their style of music has evolved from the early days and they also collaborate with many famous artists.

(48) **7** Maroon 5's **promotional videos** are very popular, too. Some of them almost seem like movies, with Adam Levine as the star. In fact, he can act quite well and has appeared in several real movies.

8 Listening to Maroon 5 songs is a great way to study English. Check out their songs on YouTube!

(236 words)

Adam Levine	アダム・レヴィーン
lead singer	ヴォーカル
hit	ヒット曲
single	シングル盤
debut album	デビューアルバム
promotional video	プロモーションビデオ

 **Pair Work** 下線部が何を指しているかパートナーと一緒に考えましょう。

True or False ▶ 本文の内容と一致すれば **T**（True）を、一致しなければ **F**（False）を記入しましょう。

（　）１．Maroon 5 is a British band.
（　）２．The number of members has decreased.
（　）３．Maroon 5's lead singer has a deep voice.
（　）４．"This Love" is a song about finding a new girlfriend.
（　）５．Maroon 5's first album was successful.
（　）６．Not all of their singles have been successful.
（　）７．Adam Levine is also an actor.
（　）８．Maroon 5 songs can be seen on YouTube.

Collocation

空欄を埋め意味の通る英文にしましょう。

1. I am happy to hear (　　　　　) her passing the examination.　（〜について聞く）
2. This book is based (　　　　) a true story.　（〜に基づいて）
3. The prices of vegetables have gone (　　　　　　　　) recently.　（上下する）
4. We often collaborate (　　　　　) local people to do research.　（〜と協力して）
5. Let's check (　　　　) the new fashions in Shibuya.　（〜を調べる）

Vocabulary Quiz

空欄に ⋯⋯ の語を入れて、和文と同じ意味の英文にしましょう。

actually	appeared	distinctive	evolve
expanded	lyrics	originally	relationship

1. To maintain a good (　　　　　　　　) with my friends, I keep in touch with them.　友人と良い関係を保つために、私は彼らと連絡をとり続けている。

2. She speaks modestly, but (　　　　　　) she is very stubborn.
彼女は穏やかに話すが実際はとても頑固だ。

3. After the actress (　　　　　　) in a drama, she became popular.
その女優はあるドラマに出た後、人気者になった。

4. This convenience store was (　　　　　　) a restaurant.
このコンビニは元々はレストランだった。

5. Our chain of shops has (　　　　　　) to fourteen branches.
私達のチェーン店は 14 店舗に拡大した。

6. How will humans (　　　　　　) in the future?
将来、人間はどのように進化するだろう？

7. This singer isn't good at writing happy (　　　　　　).
この歌手は楽しい歌詞を書くのが下手だ。

8. *Natto* has a (　　　　　　) flavor.
納豆には独特の香りがある。

Reading Summary

下記の日本語をヒントにして空欄に当てはまる語（1語とは限りません）を入れ、本文の要約を完成させましょう。必要なら辞書を使いましょう。

One of the most popular bands in America is Maroon 5. This band (　　　　　　　　　　) in California around 2001 and continues to have hits today. The band has a charismatic vocalist, Adam Levine, who is (　　　　　　　　　) for his high-pitched voice. Their first album was a big (　　　　　　　　　) around the world and several of the songs became hit singles. More albums and singles have (   ). Not all of their songs have been hits, but this band works very (   ). Even if one of their singles is not so popular, they do not (   ). Indeed, recently they have had several big hits. Many of their fans enjoy their promotional videos, which sometimes seem like short movies. If you are (   ), they are all (   ) on YouTube.

諦める	後に続いた	興味がある	結成された
成功	入手可能な	熱心に	よく知られている

Grammar Point + Grammar Exercise

 現在完了形

例 Maroon 5 **has** now **expanded** to seven members.
Since 2004, Maroon 5's popularity **has gone** up and down.
Some of their singles **have been** hits, while others were not so popular.
Their style of music **has evolved** from the early days and they also collaborate with many famous artists.
He can act quite well and **has appeared** in several real movies.

いっしょに使われる語句に注意しましょう。
- （すでに）〜した、（ちょうど）〜したところだ 【already, just, yet】
- 〜したことがある 【once, twice, 〜 times, never, ever】
- （〜以来、〜の期間）〜している 【since, for】

現在完了に注意して、次の英文を日本語にしましょう。
1. I have been to Tokyo Disneyland more than twenty times.
2. She has lived in New York for a year.
3. Have you done your homework yet?
4. It has been raining heavily since last Saturday.
5. The meeting has just ended. Don't be late next time.

Unit 13 Walking and Talking

Pre-Reading Questions

1 Do you often use earphones with your smartphone?

2 What type of earphones do you use? Take them out now and show your classmates and teacher. Why did you choose that type?

(49) Vocabulary Task ▷ 英単語とその日本語の意味を結び付けましょう。

1. whole	( )	a. 保護、防護物
2. embarrassed	( )	b. 近づく
3. protection	( )	c. おしゃべりする
4. hesitate	( )	d. 全体の
5. approach	( )	e. 盗む
6. robber	( )	f. 恥ずかしい
7. steal	( )	g. ためらう
8. chat	( )	h. 泥棒

上記の語を本文中から見つけて○をつけましょう。

(50) Reading

NOTES

1 Recently, we often see young people walking around town, talking to <u>themselves</u>. Some older people might wonder, "Are they OK?!"

2 Of course, <u>they</u> are not talking to themselves. They are using

54

their **wireless earphones** and smartphone to make a phone call to a friend or family member.

❸ One reason this has become popular is because of new types of earphones, such as the Apple **AirPods**.

❹ These wireless earphones are very convenient. Not only are <u>they</u> great for music, they are also good for phone calls.

❺ AirPods have a microphone, so you can use the **voice assistant Siri** to make and take calls. In fact, you never have to take your smartphone out of your pocket or bag. You can control the whole process by voice.

❻ **In the past**, many people were embarrassed to do <u>this</u>. However, these days, young people seem **less shy**.

❼ For women coming home late at night, talking on the phone with earphones can be a kind of protection. A bad person may hesitate to approach. Also, because the smartphone is in the pocket or bag, a robber cannot easily steal <u>it</u>.

❽ Many young people also think that chatting while walking makes the best use of time. While walking from your home to the station, for example, you can call friends and make plans. It can make the walk more interesting.

❾ Do you walk and talk?

(229 words)

wireless earphone
ワイアレスイアフォン
AirPods
エアポッド（アップル社のワイヤレスイヤホン）

voice assistant
音声アシスタント
Siri
シリ（アップル社の音声アシスタント）

in the past
過去に
less shy
（劣等比較）以前ほど恥ずかしがり屋ではない

 **Pair Work** 下線部が何を指しているかパートナーと一緒に考えましょう。

True or False

本文の内容と一致すれば **T**（True）を、一致しなければ **F**（False）を記入しましょう。

( ) 1. Some young people talk on phones while walking.
( ) 2. Some wireless earphones are good for phone calls.
( ) 3. You must connect a microphone to AirPods.
( ) 4. The process is controlled by head movements.
( ) 5. Young people are not so shy these days.
( ) 6. Walking and talking might help protect women at night.
( ) 7. Walking and talking may be good time management.
( ) 8. Many young people do it on the train to make plans.

Collocation ▷

日本語をヒントに空欄を埋め意味のとおる英文にしましょう。

1. My six-month-old baby boy seems to talk to (　　　　　　　) sometimes.

   (独り言を言う)

2. My husband always (　　　　　) a phone call to me from his office before
   coming home.　　　　　　　　　　　　　　　　　　(〜に電話をかける)

3. I'll be out this afternoon. Could you (　　　　　) a call for me?　(電話に出る)

4. First, please take the product (　　　　　　) the box.　(〜から取り出す)

5. We should make the best (　　　　) of old items by selling them online.

   (〜の利点を活かす)

Vocabulary Quiz ▷

空欄に [:::::] の語を入れて、和文と同じ意味の英文にしましょう。

| approaching | chat | embarrassed | hesitate |
| protection | robber | steal | whole |

1. This year's strongest typhoon is (　　　　　　　　) Okinawa.
   今年最大の台風が沖縄に接近中です。

2. You should take (　　　　　　　　) against the rain with you, such as an
   umbrella.　傘のような雨よけを持っていくべきだ。

3. Be careful. Bad people sometimes (　　　　　　　) bicycles in this area.
   注意してください。悪い人々は時々この地域で自電車を盗みます。

4. The rumor spread rapidly across the (　　　　　) country.
   うわさが急速に国中に広がった。

5. The (　　　　　　) was captured by the police some days after his escape.
   泥棒は数日間の逃亡の後、警察に捕まった。

6. I felt (　　　　　　　) when I carelessly wore odd socks.
   うっかり左右で違う色の靴下を履いていた時、恥ずかしく感じた。

7. It is a lot of fun to (　　　　　　) with friends online.
   ネットで友達とおしゃべりするのはとても楽しい。

8. Don't (　　　　　　) to ask me for help if necessary.
   必要なら、ためらわずに私に手助けを求めてください。

Reading Summary ▷

下記の日本語をヒントにして空欄に当てはまる語（1語とは限りません）を入れ、本文の要約を完成させましょう。必要なら辞書を使いましょう。

(　　　　　　　　　　), if we saw someone walking and　(　　　　　　　　　　),
it may have seemed strange. Now many people seem to be doing it. However, in

fact, they are not talking to themselves, they are using earphones and a smartphone to ( ). New earphones have a microphone built-in. This is great technology and the sound ( ) when chatting is good. You can control everything by ( ) so it is very convenient. You do not have to take out your smartphone. These days, young people are less self-conscious, so they do not ( ) doing it. Walking and chatting may be good for ( ), especially for women walking home ( ) at night. You can also use time efficiently by walking and making a call at the same time.

*self-conscious 自意識過剰の

安全	遅くに	気にする	過去に
声	電話をかける	独り言を言う	品質

Grammar Point + Grammar Exercise

原因と結果

例 One reason is **because of** new types of earphones, such as the Apple AirPods.
→ because of ＋語句

Because the smartphone is in the pocket or bag, a robber cannot easily steal it. → because ＋主語＋動詞

AirPods have a microphone, **so** you can use the voice assistant Siri to make and take calls. → so, therefore, as a result などは前に原因・理由が述べられています。

日本語を参考にして、適切な語（句）を入れましょう。

1. He is easily misunderstood ( ) his stubbornness.
   彼は頑固さのために誤解されやすい。

2. ( ) I got something in my eye, tears ran down my face.
   目に何かが入ったので、涙が流れた。

3. The politician caused a scandal. ( ), he will lose the next election.
   その政治家は不祥事を起こした。だから次の選挙では落選するだろう。

4. ( ) for his promotion is his popularity.
   彼の昇進の理由の１つは人望だ。

5. The big earthquake caused a blackout. ( ), I was late for work.
   大きな地震で停電が起きた。その結果、仕事に遅刻してしまいました。

Unit 14

Are You Going Cashless?

Pre-Reading Questions

1 By what percentage are you a 'cash person' and a 'cashless person'?
(for example → I am 70% cash and 30% cashless)

2 What cashless payment methods do you use?

(53) Vocabulary Task ▷ 英単語とその日本語の意味を結び付けましょう。

1. generation （ 　 ）　　a. 海外で
2. cashless （ 　 ）　　b. 購入する
3. overseas （ 　 ）　　c. 類似の
4. confusing （ 　 ）　　d. 現金不要の
5. similar （ 　 ）　　e. 物質的な
6. purchase （ 　 ）　　f. 分かりにくい
7. physical （ 　 ）　　g. 備える、保管する
8. store （ 　 ）　　h. 世代、年代

上記の語を本文中から見つけて○をつけましょう。

(54) Reading

NOTES

1 Many people in Japan still use cash, especially the older generation. For <u>them</u>, using cash feels familiar and safe.

2 The younger generation, however, are becoming **more and more** cashless. Young people like things to be convenient and

more and more ~
益々~

they also welcome new technologies.

❸ Even so, most people are probably in the '**hybrid**' stage, using cash for some things and going cashless for other things. Indeed, some shops and restaurants in Japan still only accept cash.

hybrid　混合の

(55) ❹ Overseas, the situation is different. In the United Kingdom, for example, some bars have become 'cashless only'. Customers cannot pay by cash, even if <u>they</u> want to!

❺ In Japan, there are many different ways to go cashless. The various options might be confusing.

❻ One simple way to become cashless in Japan is with a **Suica** card or similar. Just use cash to **top-up** your card and then you can use it to purchase things and to ride trains.

Suica　スイカ

top-up　つぎ足す

(56) ❼ More advanced cashless methods are smartphone **based**, such as **Apple Pay** or **Google Pay**. With <u>these</u>, you do not need **physical cards** — your cards are **digital cards**, stored in your smartphone. You can add many different types of cards to your smartphone: credit cards, Suica, and more. <u>This</u> means that you have more options for cashless payments.

~ based
〜に基づいた
Apple Pay
アップルペイ
Google Pay
グーグルペイ
physical card
クレジットカード
digital card
電子マネーカード

❽ And one more way to go cashless is to use smartphone apps such as **PayPay**, which also offer discounts and points.

PayPay　ペイペイ

❾ Are you going cashless? Which methods do you use?

(239 words)

 **Pair Work**　下線部が何を指しているかパートナーと一緒に考えましょう。

True or False ▶ 本文の内容と一致すれば **T** (True) を、一致しなければ **F** (False) を記入しましょう。

(　) 1．Old people prefer cashless payment methods.
(　) 2．Young people like cashless payment methods.
(　) 3．Some shops in Japan are now 'cashless only'.
(　) 4．In some bars in the UK, you cannot use cash.
(　) 5．Japan has many cashless payment methods.
(　) 6．Using a Suica card for cashless payments is difficult.
(　) 7．With Apple Pay, you can pay with various cards.
(　) 8．PayPay is a smart card that offers discounts.

Unit 14

Collocation

日本語をヒントに空欄を埋め意味の通る英文にしましょう。

1. Many people (＿＿＿＿＿＿＿) cashless these days. （キャッシュレスにする）
2. Some shops (＿＿＿＿＿＿＿＿) cash. （現金を受け付ける）
3. Can I pay (＿＿＿＿＿＿＿) cash? （現金で払う）
4. I always add two spoons of sugar (＿＿＿＿＿＿) my coffee. （～に…を加える）
5. There are many options (＿＿＿＿＿) eating out in my local area. （～の選択肢）

Vocabulary Quiz

空欄に ⬚ の語を入れて、和文と同じ意味の英文にしましょう。

> | | | | |
> |---|---|---|---|
> | cashless | confusing | generation | overseas |
> | physical | purchase | similar | store |

1. My sister is busy with preparing for studying (＿＿＿＿＿＿＿).
   姉は海外留学の準備で忙しい。
2. For Japanese people, "think" and "sink" sound quite (＿＿＿＿＿＿＿).
   日本人には think と sink はかなり似ているように聞こえる。
3. This dress was in vogue a (＿＿＿＿＿＿＿) ago.
   このワンピースは一世代前に流行った。
4. The (＿＿＿＿＿＿＿) size of computers is becoming smaller, but they are becoming more powerful.
   コンピュータの物理的な大きさはより小さくなっているが、さらに強力になっている。
5. Some animals (＿＿＿＿＿＿＿) food for winter.
   ある動物たちは冬に備えて食料を蓄える。
6. I think a (＿＿＿＿＿＿＿) society is not good for people who are careless about money. 現金不要の社会はお金に無頓着な人にとっては良くないと思います。
7. You should avoid using (＿＿＿＿＿＿＿) expressions in an emergency.
   緊急時には分かりにくい表現は避けるべきだ。
8. Do you (＿＿＿＿＿＿＿) shoes on the Internet?
   ネットで靴を購入しますか。

Reading Summary

下記の日本語をヒントにして空欄に当てはまる語（1語とは限りません）を入れ、本文の要約を完成させましょう。必要なら辞書を使いましょう。

In Japan, older people still mainly use cash. However, (＿＿＿＿＿＿＿＿＿＿＿) payment methods are gradually becoming more popular, especially with the younger (＿＿＿＿＿＿＿＿＿). Certainly, a cashless society fits with younger people's lifestyles. In other countries, cashless payments may be even more popular than

Japan. In Europe, some bars only （ 　　　　　　　　） cards or smartphone payments. For young people, no problem, but for older people this might be a shock. In Japan, there are many （ 　　　　　　　） go cashless. IC cards such as Suica cards are an easy way. You can use these cards to ride on a train and also pay for things at a （ 　　　　　　　　） or buy things from a （ 　　　　　　　　）. However, probably the most （ 　　　　　　　） method is to use a smartphone. Apple Pay and Google Pay are becoming very popular, （ 　　　　　　　） apps such as PayPay.

受け付ける	現金不要の	コンビニ	世代
自動販売機	～する方法	～と同様に	便利な

Grammar Point ＋ Grammar Exercise

例示の仕方

例 In the United Kingdom, **for example**, some bars have become 'cashless only'. One more way to go cashless is to use smartphone apps **such as** PayPay.

like	「～のような」　類似の事柄や似ているものを挙げる
such as	「～のような」　ある事柄の具体例や細分化された例をあげ、文頭には使えない
for example	「たとえば」　文頭にも使える
for instance	「たとえば」　実際に行われた実例をあげる
to give an example	「一例をあげると」
to name a few	「2、3の例をあげると」

下線部に注意して、次の英文を和訳しましょう。

1. We have many attractions in this amusement park: the largest Ferris wheel in Japan, a roller coaster, and bungee jumping, <u>to name a few</u>.
2. I want to be a nurse <u>like</u> my grandmother in the future.
3. There are some very small countries in Europe, <u>such as</u> Luxembourg and Monaco.
4. I like classical music, especially romantic music. <u>For example</u>, Chopin, Liszt, and Mahler.
5. I tried hard to lose weight, <u>for instance</u>, by eating low-calorie foods, walking for an hour every day, and joining a gym.

Unit 15 — Shibuya Halloween

Pre-Reading Questions

1 What is your favorite Western festival?
(Christmas, Valentine's Day, Halloween, etc.?)

2 Have you dressed up in a costume on Halloween or on another day?
(please include the time when you were a child!)

🎧57 Vocabulary Task ▷ 英単語とその日本語の意味を結び付けましょう。

1. atmosphere ( )		a. 横転させる
2. gather ( )		b. 雰囲気
3. overturn ( )		c. （良いものを悪くして）台無しにする
4. ban ( )		d. 同情、残念な気持ち
5. celebration ( )		e. 集まる
6. pity ( )		f. 禁止する
7. spoil ( )		g. （直せないほど）台無しにする
8. ruin ( )		h. お祝い

上記の語を本文中から見つけて〇をつけましょう。

🎧58 Reading

❶ Halloween is a fun event. <u>It</u> is a chance to dress up, meet friends and enjoy the **spooky** Halloween atmosphere.

❷ In Tokyo, many young people gather in Shibuya at Halloween.

NOTES

spooky 不気味な

The amazing costumes that some people wear have made the Shibuya Halloween famous around the world.

(59) ❸ Sometimes there have been problems, though. One year, some **rowdy** young men overturned a small truck in Shibuya at Halloween. As a result, drinking alcohol has been banned in the area during the Halloween celebrations.

❹ Perhaps the Shibuya Halloween is a little **less lively** now. It is a pity. Just a few **troublemakers** can spoil things for everybody.

❺ But there may also be another problem.

❻ Because the Shibuya Halloween has become famous, many people come to see it, both Japanese and foreign visitors. However, most of these visitors do not dress up!

(60) ❼ Above all, Halloween is a time for wearing a costume. Many young people who come to Shibuya make a big effort to dress up as **zombies**, **vampires**, **monsters** and many more characters. It is a wonderful aspect of this celebration.

❽ But if most people are not dressing up, it ruins the party. They seem like **freeloaders**, just taking photos of people in costumes, but doing nothing themselves.

❾ So perhaps Shibuya needs a new Halloween rule... **no costume, no entry**!

(217 words)

rowdy [ráudi]
乱暴な

less lively
それほど活気がない
troublemakers
悶着を起こす人

zombies
(zombie の複数形)
ゾンビ
vampire 吸血鬼
monsters 怪物
freeloader
ただ乗りする人、
たかり屋
no A, no B　A が
なければ B もない
entry　入場

Pair Work　下線部が何を指しているかパートナーと一緒に考えましょう。

True or False

本文の内容と一致すれば **T** (True) を、一致しなければ **F** (False) を記入しましょう。

( ) 1. Young people gather in Shibuya at Halloween.
( ) 2. Foreign people do not know about the Shibuya Halloween.
( ) 3. One year, some rowdy men stole a truck.
( ) 4. Drinking alcohol is permitted in Shibuya at Halloween.
( ) 5. Japanese and foreign people come to Shibuya at Halloween.
( ) 6. Young people do their best to make great costumes.
( ) 7. Zombies, vampires and monsters are ruining the party.
( ) 8. There is now a new rule... no costume, no entry.

Unit 15

Collocation

日本語をヒントに空欄を埋め意味の通る英文にしましょう。

1. Let's dress (　　　　　) for the graduation party. （正装する）

2. My parents were strict. (　　　　　　　) all, they demanded good manners.

（とりわけ）

3. Christmas is a time (　　　　　) exchanging presents. （〜の時期）

4. She (　　　　　　) an effort to keep a good score. （〜する努力をする）

5. The actors appeared (　　　　　) costumes for the performance. （〜を着て）

Vocabulary Quiz

空欄に 　　 の語を入れて、和文と同じ意味の英文にしましょう。

atmosphere	banned	celebration	gathered
overturned	pity	ruined	spoils

1. The decision was (　　　　　　　　　) by the company president.
   その決定は会社社長によって否決された。

2. It was a (　　　　　　) that the barbecue was cancelled.
   バーベキューパーティが中止になったのは残念だ。

3. The bad weather (　　　　　　　) my plans for a hiking trip.
   悪天候で私のハイキングの計画が台無しになった。

4. A lot of people (　　　　　　) to protest against the tax increase.
   大勢の人々が増税に抗議するために集まった。

5. The company will hold a (　　　　　　　) for the 100th anniversary of its
   foundation next year. その会社は来年、設立100周年のお祝いを開くだろう。

6. I like the lively (　　　　　　　) of this restaurant.
   私はこのレストランの活気ある雰囲気が好きだ。

7. The new building next to the historic shrine (　　　　　) the view.
   由緒ある神社の隣の新しい建物は景観を台無しにしている。

8. You must remember that smoking is (　　　　　) at a gas station.
   ガソリンスタンドでは喫煙は禁止されていることを覚えておかなければならない。

Reading Summary

下記の日本語をヒントにして空欄に当てはまる語（1語とは限りません）を入れ、本文の要約を完成させましょう。必要なら辞書を使いましょう。

In recent years, Shibuya has become a popular place for young people to
(　　　　　　　　) at Halloween. There is a party (　　　　　　　　　　)
and many youngsters like to dress up (　　　　　　　　) to get in the mood.
Zombies and various other (　　　　　　　　) creatures can be seen walking

around Shibuya during the Halloween season. However, some young people have been too rowdy and, in one incident, a small truck was damaged. Now, alcohol (　　　　　　　　　　　　). Another recent trend has been for more and more visitors to come to the Shibuya Halloween, hoping to see people in fantastic costumes. However, these visitors do not dress up themselves. They merely　(　　　　　　　　　　). Some people　(　　　　　　　　) that a new rule is needed — if you don't wear a costume, you cannot　(　　　　　　　) the party.

集まる	禁止されている	コスチュームを着て	怖い
参加する	写真を撮る	提案した	雰囲気

Grammar Point + Grammar Exercise

 相関接続詞

㋑ Many people come to see it, **both** Japanese **and** foreign visitors.

both A and B	「A と B の両方」	主語になった場合、動詞は複数扱いになる
either A or B	「A か B のどちらか」	主語になった場合、動詞は B の数に一致
neither A nor B	「A も B も〜ない」	主語になった場合、動詞は B の数に一致

日本語を参考にして、空欄に上記の中から適切な語、または be 動詞を入れましょう。

1. He (　　　　　　　　) reads newspapers (　　　　　　　　) watches news programs.
   彼は新聞も読まないしニュース番組も見ない。

2. You can play (　　　　　　) soccer (　　　　　　) basketball for PE class.
   あなたたちは体育の授業でサッカーかバスケットボールのどちらかができます。

3. My mother can speak (　　　　　　) English (　　　　) French.
   私の母は英語もフランス語も話せます。

4. Either you or he (　　　　　) wrong.
   あなたか彼のどちらかが間違っています。

5. Both he and I (　　　　) in New York last week.
   先週、彼も私もニューヨークにいました。

著者

Jonathan Lynch（ジョナサン・リンチ）

山本　厚子（やまもと　あつこ）

渡辺香名子（わたなべ　かなこ）

［入門］考える基礎英語読本

2021年2月20日　　第1版発行
2022年2月20日　　第4版発行

著　者 —— Jonathan Lynch／山本厚子／渡辺香名子

発行者 —— 前田俊秀

発行所 —— 株式会社　三修社

〒150-0001　東京都渋谷区神宮前2-2-22
TEL 03-3405-4511 / FAX 03-3405-4522
振替 00190-9-72758
https://www.sanshusha.co.jp
編集担当　三井るり子

印刷所 —— 倉敷印刷株式会社

©2021 Printed in Japan ISBN978-4-384-33502-6 C1082

表 紙 デ ザ イ ン —— SAIWAI Design（山内宏一郎）
本文デザイン・DTP —— ME TIME LLC（大貫としみ）
準 拠 音 声 制 作 —— 高速録音株式会社
準 拠 音 声 録 音 —— ELEC（吹込：Rachel Walzer / Neil DeMaere）

教科書準拠CD発売

本書の準拠CDをご希望の方は弊社までお問い合わせください。